Locanda dell'Amorosa (Photo Vincent Gyselinck)

With special thanks to our photographers

Jan Dirkx
Vincent Gyselinck
Patrick Verbeeck

&

Paul Kusseneers

Concept & Lay-Out

&

Printed by de plano

> More information on all our books you find on our website :
> **www.d-publications.com**

Compiled by: Luc Quisenaerts
Concept & lay-out: Paul Kusseneers
Printed by: De Plano
Pre-press: Paul Kusseneers
Texts: Anne & Owen Davis
English translation: Anne & Owen Davis

List of photographers:
<u>Jan Dirkx</u> : Hotel J&J, Villa San Michele, Salvadonica, Villa Vignamaggio, Borgo Argenino, Lucignanello Bandini, l'Antico Pozzo, La Collegiata, Il Pelicano.
<u>Vincent Gyselinck</u> : Castello di Montegufoni, Helvetia & Bristol, Villa La Massa, Certosa di Maggiano, Relais La Suvera, Villa Arceno, Locanda dell'Amorosa, Castelletto di Montebenichi.
<u>Patrick Verbeeck</u> : Il Bottaccio di Montignoso, Locanda l'Elisa, L'Olmo, Castello di Magona, La Frateria di Padre Eligio, Il Falconiere, Gallery Hotel Art, Lungarno.
<u>Karel Daems</u> : Castello di Montegufoni

ISBN 90-76124-32-9   D/2000/8101/5

© All rights reserved. No part of this publication may be reproduced in any way whatsoever without written permission from D-Publications.

First edition

Hidden gems of
TUSCANY

COMPILED BY
LUC QUISENAERTS

WRITTEN BY

ANNE & OWEN DAVIS

PUBLISHERS D-PUBLICATIONS

THE SERIES
Hidden gems

Dear reader,

In this series, we take you to the most wonderful places to stay, to eat and to enjoy the specialties of a country or an area.

Every article in this series is a journey of discovery, a unique revelation. We take a look behind the scenes in a hotel, a wine chateau, a restaurant where we savour the specialties of the chef or of the area…

With this series, we intend to give the readers the opportunity to leaf through each book and 'walk' through these wonderful spots, and discover the unique nooks and crannies of each of them.

Therefore this series, and each volume in itself, can be considered a valuable archive which brings a piece of the richness and beauty of an area or country into the home, created and cherished by the passion of the people who put part souls into it.

In word and photographs, the typical atmosphere of each place is conjured, and each book can be considered the 'key' to a wonderful and often undiscovered world.

The selection was made and approved of by the publisher himself, which guarantees it to be a unique experience, with unforgettable impressions of what our hosts have to offer.

. . .

Hidden gems of TUSCANY

In this book, we visit hotels that once were Tuscan villages, and superb villas in the most idyllic locations, amongst vineyards in the beautiful Chianti region.

We stay in former the homes of the Medici family and in monasteries that are centuries old; in a small palazzo within the walls of San Gimignano; in ancient castles where everything is just like it used to be, including the furniture; in the home of rich Florentine families on the river Arno, surrounded by cypresses, and in a vineyard where, in the 15th century, the woman was born who became known as the Mona Lisa.

We dine on terraces by candlelight, enjoying the balmy summer air, surrounded by landscapes reminiscent of the great Renaissance paintings.

And finally, we discover Florence, where we stay in design hotels and in more traditional houses with all the grandeur of the 19th century. And last but not least, we discover a villa in the hills of Fiesole, and admire the work of Michelangelo.

Luc Quisenaerts
Publisher

THE COLLECTION

	Pag.
Relais Il Falconiere	10
Salvadonica	18
Castelletto di Montebenichi	24
L'Antico Pozzo	30
Lucignanello Bandini	34
L'Olmo	42
Lungarno	48
Il Botaccio di Montignoso	54
Villa La Massa	60
Borgo Argenina	68
Locanda l'Elisa	76
La Collegiata	80
Il Pellicano	86
Relais La Suvera	92
Castello di Magona	100
Certosa di Maggiano	108
La Frateria di Padre Eligio	116
Gallery Hotel Art	122
Villa San Michele	128
Relais Villa Arceno	134
Helvetia & Bristol	140
Castello di Montegufoni	146
Hotel J & J	154
Locanda dell'Amorosa	158
Villa Vignamaggio	166

Relais Il Falconiere

The province of Arezzo lies upstream from Florence, reached by the valley of the Arno, a busy thoroughfare which carries the main rail link from Florence to Rome and the Autostrada del Sole.

But you could avoid all this by turning off onto the forested and hilly N70 through Vallombrosa and then Poppi, along the Pratomagno bridge, around the side of Monte Secchieta, a winter ski resort but lovely, too, in summer and a walker's paradise.

There'll be plenty of gear-changing and lots of bends, but some wonderful views, too, across Chianti country that make this detour well worth it, if you have the time.

Arezzo is famous for the lovely frescoes by Piero della Francesca, illustrating the Legend of the Cross, to be found in the otherwise unappealing Basilica San Francesco. South of Arezzo is the flat cattle country of the Valdichiana. Attractive Cortona stands on a solitary hilltop, reached by a winding road through terraced vineyards and groves of ancient olives: a visit for the views is a must.

But don't stay overnight in either Arezzo or Cortona. Two short miles outside Cortona is a serene and lovely hotel, Il Falconiere, and this is where you should head for. There are frescoes here, too; not by the celebrated Piero, but very fetching and romantic none the less.

Run by an engaging and very welcoming young couple, Sylvia and Riccardo Barachi, Il Falconiere is a castle-like and dramatic 16th-century villa, guarded by tall soldier-straight cypresses and reached by an avenue of mature and enveloping horse chestnuts.

Sylvia and Riccardo have restored the building most beautifully and added a sparkling and spacious conservatory at one end, and an equally sun-drenched and inviting swimming-pool awaits the dusty traveller in the gorgeous gardens.

In the 19th century, Il Falconiere was the home of Italian poet Antonio Guadagnoli; much loved even today in his homeland, and there is poetry still in the 12 wooden-beamed suites, with their four-poster beds, frescoes, oriental rugs, vases of fresh flowers and extensive views.

All this is reason enough to seek out this seductive Relais et Châteaux hotel; but the cuisine at Il Falconiere is very special, too. The restaurant is situated on two floors, in the ancient 'lemon house' and in the peaceful evenings of summertime Tuscany, it spills out onto the rose-arboured terrace.

The tables are beautifully set, with tall candle-lights throwing a living glow onto the twinkling silver and prestine linen. The chef, with the support of Sylvia herself, prepares a whole selection of marvellously original recipes, firmly rooted nevertheless in the authentic flavours of old Tuscany. Sylvia has taken much care, too, over the wine list: it would be worth asking for some advice - you may be introduced to some great wines you were unfamiliar with.

Salvadonica

Salvadonica lies halfway between Florence and Siena, in the Chianti region. Chianti is probably many a European's idea of an earthly paradise: a balmy climate most of the year, landscapes worthy, even today, of the great Renaissance masters, romantic and wonderfully preserved medieval towns and hilltop villages... and great wines at every turn.

If you head for Chianti country southwards from Florence, you can forego the highway and choose the meandering Route SSN2, through the western edges of Chianti, or the SSN3, a little further east, which dives right into the hilly Chianti heartland. You can go from one interesting town to another, and stop for lunch or turn off anywhere to visit vineyards on right or left, and be welcomed there. The estate of Salvadonica combines a working farm with a range of luxury holiday apartments, spread across several farmhouses and villas. It boldly calls itself a 'burgo agrituristico' and visitors are encouraged to take an interest in all that goes on around them, which can give their holiday in Tuscany an extra dimen-

sion. Nice as it is to view great art on gallery walls, it can be a relief to rejoin the present. At Salvadonica, there is a tennis court, a bowling green, and - set a little apart - a wonderfully welcoming swimming-pool. Nearby, only yards beyond the estate boundary, horseriders will find a stables... and all the acres of countryside around is waiting to be enjoyed on horseback.

The guest rooms are comfortable and spacious, with cosy modern bathrooms and well-equipped kitchens for self-catering. But you can also eat at any one of dozens of good restaurants just waiting to be discovered as you explore the surrounding area.

When you leave Salvadonica, be sure to buy a few bottles of the wine produced on the estate. By then, you will have discovered your own favourite: the Classico, the Capovolto or the Donico... or there's the extra virgin olive oil, in its elegantly slim long-necked bottle. Wonderful souvenirs of an equally wonderful holiday!

Castelletto di Montebenichi

Montebenichi is one of a network of fortresses built on a strategic line of defence along the edge of the Chianti region in the Valdambra, between ancient Siena and Arezzo...

It is an unforgettable experience to spend some time in such a castle, with its venerable history going back almost 1,000 years, to a time when Italy was a rough-hewn collection of embattled city states, always bickering if not in a state of outright conflict.

It has, of course, been completely restored and is supremely comfortable now, as well as imposing. The cool, luxurious rooms are fit for counts and contessas and as I gazed from my window, I felt enormously privileged and pampered.

Today there are no Florentine troops beseiging Montebenichi. The pretty, well-tended, rolling countryside stretching away in all directions is a peaceful and serene mix of olive groves, farmland, woods and vineyards, dotted with captivating little villages and engaging market towns.

The great tourist centres of medieval Siena and Florence are close enough to reach for a day's visit, so Montebenichi makes an excellent base for the visitor who wants the best of both worlds, a little culture and a little peace and quiet, a couple of hours with the paintings of Botticelli and a couple more sitting on the vine-shaded terrace of a cafe with a coffee. Everywhere you go you'll discover perfect out-of-the-way restaurants serving excellent Tuscan food, prepared in the traditional manner.

I spent two fascinating days here just investigating the vineyards and stocking up on wine, and two more days visiting romantic and welcoming villages and peering into the dark-shadowed incense-scented naves of ancient churches.

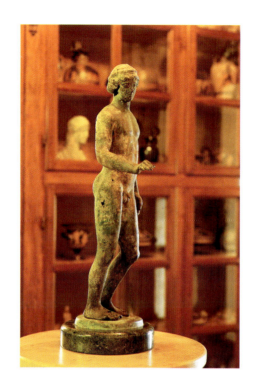

Time seemed to stand still, but eventually I had to drag myself away from the magical lands of the Valdambra back to the modern world. Thanks to Castelletto di Montebenichi, I was laden, not just with good wines to see me through the long northern winter ahead, but with many unforgettable memories.

L'Antico Pozzo

I first encountered San Gimignano not in any tourist brochure, but in a lovely book for children: And So My Garden Grows by Peter Spier, which I read to my children, enjoying it, I suspect, more than they did. The magic of the illustrations and the simple text have remained with me. In all the years since discovering that book, I had not, until now, ever found my way to "*San Gimignano delle belle torri*". It was, of course, the watercolour pictures of the incredible skyline of ancient towers that fascinated me most - and to see them in real life was like meeting old friends.

Thousands of others, too, are attracted to San Gimignano, and in high summer it is as thronged, almost, as Florence. But there are two simple tricks, if you would like to taste the medieval romance of this spectacular village without sharing the occasion with too many others: stay overnight, or come very early or late in the season; or if you can do both, so much the better.

San Gimignano is a daytime trip for visitors staying in Siena, and at sundown, happily, they are carried away on their coaches. You will find the village you hoped for, then. So, you should stay in the village itself, and within its walls.

A place I can highly recommend is the lovely three-star hotel L'Antico Pozzo, a completely refurbished and elegant 15th century town house on Via San Matteo, San Gimignano's High Street.

There are only 18 rooms and they fill quickly, so I suggest you book well ahead. By the way, it shuts its doors for the winter months.

The earliest parts of the building go back to the Middle Ages. For over 200 years, it was the home of a religious order, then found new and secular life as a haunt of high society. The restoration has clearly been carried out with great sympathy for its past history... and it doesn't take much imagination, when the alleyways outside are empty of people, to feel yourself transported back in time.

E.M. Forster's book Where Angels Fear to Tread is set in San Gimignano, and it is not hard to imagine those angels in such a beautiful environment.

But there are real benefits in travelling swiftly back to the present day. L'Antico Pozzo is magnificently comfortable and you'll find all those modern conveniences that are, in their welcoming way, just as magical as the past: air-conditioning, satellite television, a cosy bar and a heavenly room at bedtime, where I lay and watched a full moon make its way carefully between San Gimignano's medieval towers. Were I to go back to Peter Spier's book, perhaps I might find myself more critical: I will find he makes no mention of our new secret, the splendid Hotel L'Antico Pozzo.

Lucignanello Bandini

I have written many times about castles, villas and town houses that have been beautifully and painstakingly restored, to find new life as desirable hotels for the discerning traveller, but never before of an entire village being given the same kind of makeover.
Lucignano d'Asso, in the southernmost part of Tuscany, is an hour's drive from Siena - but you'll need a good map to help you find your way through the undulating rural landscape of wheatfields and olive groves, vineyards and leafy oak woodlands to this discreet hamlet, set apart from the world and dedicated, in its serene entirety, to the needs of the visitor to this special part of Europe.

The scale of the project and its stern promise to truly reflect Lucignano's historical identity demanded a knowledgeable consultant, and Paolo Rossi, one of Italy's foremost experts in architectural restoration, was called in to oversee the work.

As well as the guest houses, painted in gentle pastels of pink, pale ochre and beige, and accommodating from four to six people each, Lucignano has its own castle, two pretty churches and, you'll be relieved to learn, its own little shop.

The same careful attention to detail has also been lavished on the interiors. Furnishings were selected by Vera Marzot, costume designer to Italian opera houses. Warm hues of terracotta, seasoned wood, hand-painted ceramics and bright cottons abound.

There are five finely-appointed casas to choose from, each of them a jewel, and, set at a little distance away, a large traditional farmhouse, with two verandahs and its own swimming-pool, overlooked by a romantic pergola with table and chairs for al fresco dining.

If you can drag yourself away from your home at Lucignano d'Asso, there are, close by, two villages of stunning beauty and historial significance you should visit - and you could walk to them. Peaceful, affluent Montalcino is the classic model of a Tuscan walled hill-town, with a lovely castle standing guard, and Pienza, similarly, is a Renaissance gem with incredible views.

If you've already stood before the great Italian paintings in Florence and Siena, then a spell in this bucolic scenery will seem as if you have entered, by way of some magic door, into the very soul of the Renaissance.

L'Olmo

As I travel through what must surely be one of Europe's most seductive and beautiful regions, I have been captivated not only by the gorgeous scenery, but also by the amount of small but jewel-like hotels waiting to be discovered in out-of-the-way corners at every turn of the road.

L'Olmo (which translates, quite simply, as the Elm), is set in the depths of the quiet and still totally unspoilt Monticchiello region of Val'Orcia in southern Tuscany, and is another perfect example. Originally a generously-proportioned gentleman's country farmhouse, built in the 17th century, L'Olmo has been beautifully restored and offers just five luxury suites and one double room.

The wooden-beamed suites, each of them very characterful and suprisingly different from one another, have a cosy bedroom with a four-poster bed, a lounge furnished with grand antiques and a luxurious bathroom. From every suite, there are wonderful views of the spectacular sculptural scenery, spreading far into the distance. If you're fortunate enough to secure one of the two ground floor suites, you'll have your own private secluded garden, too, and a jacuzzi.

When you leave your suite, you'll discover a friendly lounge and a nicely-appointed dining room for your leisurely breakfast in the morning and for dinner in the evening (cooked, at your request, by the owner Francesca Lindo

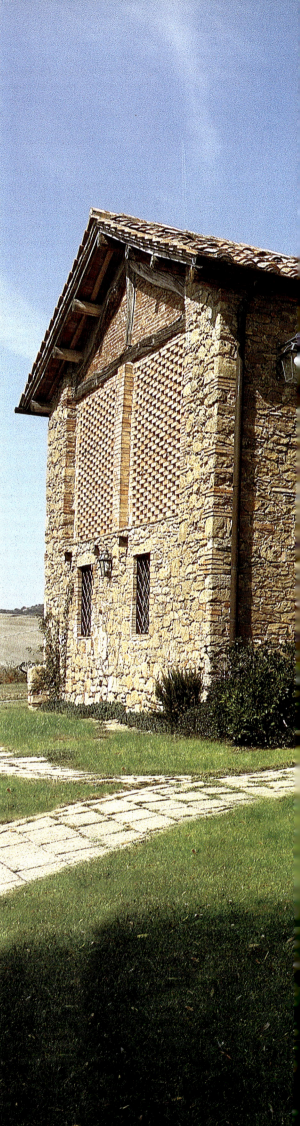

herself). Outside, there's a poetic stone-flagged arched typically Tuscan courtyard, and real sun-trap… and for those hot and cloudless summer days an inviting twinkling aquamarine swimming-pool.

There is plenty in the surrounding area to divert and intrigue the visitor. For myself, I loved the old track that leads you eastwards to Monticchiello, a gentle stroll away, and then continues onwards to Montepulciano. It is undemanding exercise and, if you time it right, you can reward yourself in Monticchiello with an excellent lunch at the Taverna di Morando and a lingering cappuccino and pastry later on in one of the lovely little squares in beautifully-named Montepulciano, Tuscany's highest medieval hilltop village. Everywhere you look are wonderfully preserved Renaissance churches and palazzi.

As the late afternoon sun gradually sinks towards the horizon, you could, I think, allow yourself a bus or a taxi home to L'Olmo and one of Signora Francesca's gourmet dinnners. You will leave eventually - but forsake, too, a little bit of your heart, and without regret. You can always return to reclaim it on a future visit to L'Olmo.

Hotel Lungarno

The origins of the city of Florence go back far beyond the Roman Empire to the Etruscans, who founded Fiesole on a nearby hill, for its defensive position, and sent only a small group down to the riverside to set up a modest village where the great city now stands.

The great floods of 1966 were only one of many vicissitudes that have beset Florence over two millenia and more. This date is significant in the story of one of Florence's best hotels, the Lungarno; optimistically, it opened its doors immediately after the flood waters had receded.

For over 30 years, the Hotel Lungarno was one of the city's leading establishments. In 1997, it was comprehensively restored and now has 69 luxurious rooms and 12 charming suites, each of them an oasis of elegance and charm, an ideal refuge after a long day in the beautiful city. The Lungarno is placed conveniently on the banks of the River Arno, midway between the spectacular Ponte Vecchio and its lovely neighbour, the Ponte Dan Trinita. Like its sister nearby, the Gallery Hotel Art, the Lungarno has many fine paintings on its walls -a Picasso over the grand fireplace in the entrance hall and an important collection of art from the 1940s to the 1960s.

When I reached my room on the top floor, I made my way to the window. It was five minutes till I could drag myself away from the spectacular city-scape in front of me and inspect the room, with its clever mix of the antique and the contemporary and its superbly cosy bathroom.

The Lungarno has an excellent restaurant, its plate-glass windows offering a perfect view of the Arno swirling past outside. There's a wide choice of great Tuscan recipes, using the finest and freshest of local produce, and an extensive wine list.

After my meal, I set out for the Piazza della Signoria, a place of incomparable beauty and solemn grandeur, which takes on a magical air my night: the host of statues, by Cellini, by Donatello and Giambologna, seem about to step down from their plinths. I sat down and sipped a nightcap at a cafe table, and eventually made my way back to my luxurious room at the Lungarno Hotel. Dreams like this will never fade.

Il Bottaccio di Montignoso

When you think of Tuscany, you think of the Chianti area, Florence with its surrounding hills, Siena and San Giminano. But Tuscany also stretches towards the north west, beyond the famous cities of art Lucca and Pisa, to where the Appenine Alps touch the Riviera de Levante and the Ligurian coast. There, where Tuscany and Liguria meet, in the hills that roll down to the Thyrrean Sea, we discover an old 17th-century olive oil mill, splendidly renovated and restored to its former glory, but with all modern conveniences. Everything here is refined and surprising. In the middle of the restaurant is an immense pond full of goldfish! A well-earned Michelin star and a rich collection of wines and grappas guarantees an unforgettable evening in a very original environment.

Il Bottaccio di Montignoso has only eight rooms - suites, we should say, for they are as large as apartments - richly furnished with 16th century Italian antiques and decorated with oil paintings from the Renaissance. The 'Appartamente delle Macine', the 'Mill suite', has a 17th century fireplace, a beautiful sunken bath tub and the massive oak wheel of the original mill. Il Bottaccio di Montignoso can be found a few miles from the seaside town of Forte dei Marmi, and is ideally located for a voyage of discovery through one of the most beautiful regions of Italy: the Riviera di Levante. Through the ages, this coast, which stretches from the historic harbour town of Genoa to La Spezia has been praised for its beauty. But the most beautiful of all is undoubtedly the town of Portofino, world-famous for its pastel-coloured houses grouped around an intimate harbour - a wonderful place for romantic souls. And hidden far in the mountains, surrounded by Mediterranean flora, the coast hides yet another jewel... the Cinque Terre, a number of exquisite colourful villages and little harbours, the names of which are enough to make you slip off into a reverie: Vernazza, Manarola, Riomaggiore, Porto-venere...

Villa La Massa

When you leave the centre of Florence and follow the river Arno upstream, you can see the city slowly blend into the beautiful Tuscan countryside: lovely villas amongst high cypresses in sublime gardens and olive groves and vineyards on the rolling hills. And then comes the moment, just beyond a bend in the silver river, that you first see Villa La Massa. This building, which proudly rises high above the water, dates from the time of the Medicis. It was built by the Landini family and then became the property of various Italian, English and Russian aristocratic families. In 1948, it became a luxury hotel and its unique location and the proximity of Florence enchanted many famous guests, such as Clark Gable, Churchill, Elizabeth Taylor and Richard Burton. David Bowie and Iman rented the entire villa to celebrate their wedding there! Then, dasly, in 1983, the owners of the hotel died in a car accident. The villa slowly became run down and it was put up for sale. During that time, the owners of the equally beautiful hotel Villa d'Este on Lake Como dreamt of running a series of exclusive hotels in wonderful locations all over Italy: Rome, the Amalfi coast, Venice... and Florence. A deal was quickly reached and Villa d'Este's first acquisition outside Como was a fact. Nowadays, the Villa La Massa is a true work of art. The rooms

are spread over three different villlas: 'Villa Nuova' is the main building, and offers a wonderful view of the gardens and the river. From many of the top floor rooms, you can see the dome of the Duomo and the towers of Florence. The 'Villa Vecchia' houses the restaurant 'Il Verrocchio'. This is the oldest part of the estate, dating from the 14th century. It was once an olive oil mill and the rooms are furnished in a typically Tuscan style. Everything exudes a wonderful rural charm. The villa 'Il Villino' is on the river and has only three rooms. The atmosphere here is extremely romantic and it is hard to imagine that no more than a few bends in the river away, lies a bustling, busy metropolis.

Borgo Argenina

Elena Nappa was a celebrated and successful stylist in Milan, a city at the very heart of contemporary fashion. For years she threw herself into the hedonistic lifestyle of her peers, but always treasured her brief vacations, when she would slip gratefully away from the hurly-burly. In common with so many of us, she found she'd lost her heart to Tuscany, and she dreamed of escaping there from Milan and its continual demands on her time and her spirit. At last, on discovering the little, crumbling hamlet of Argenina, on the borders of the lovely Chianti region, she resolved to take the bull by the horns… and realise her dream.

It was not always easy. But with the help of a whole slew of craftsmen and after several long years of devotion, struggle and unaccustomed manual labour, Elena achieved her ambition: Argenina was, once again, imbued with life and regained the ancient beauty that had slowly dissolved as it fell into neglect and disrepair. Elena's skills as a stylist ensured the Borgo Argenina was delightfully designed, both inside and out. The restoration adhered rigorously to the little village's historical past. And what a history it was. It was mentioned by name in documents from the year 998 as being the property of one Ricasoli Fridolfi (and what a wonderfully resonant name that is!) In the 12th century an obscure order of monks were given use of the place… and now, by the hand of Elena Nappa, visitors to Tuscany can enjoy the wonderful position of this part castello, part farmhouse and hotel.

There are only four double rooms and two luxury apartments, so at Argenina you will feel special and can be left to enjoy the solitude, the abundant and enthusiastic climbing roses, the arched ceilings, the distant views and the wide blue Tuscan skies.

All of Chianti is on your doorstep, its winding back roads, its miles and miles of enchanting woodlands, and its graceful vineyards, always happy to receive a visitor who turns up on the off-chance, unannounced.

For a special meal, Elena will be happy to direct you to the nearby Osteria del Castello, managed by Irishman Seamus O'Kelly. Borgo Argenina has always had a special relationship to this restaurant, which is, by the way, so popular that a reservation is necessary to avoid disappointment. After a wonderful dinner, accompanied by plenty of local wine, you will be glad that it is not far to your own temporary home.

Locanda l'Elisa

A charmingly named and absolutely delightful hotel awaits you in Lucca, Pisa's less renowned but equally lovely neigbour. Henry James, the American writer with something of a passion for dispatching his characters on European travel, said of Tuscany's graceful northern capital: "Lucca is a place overflowing with everything that makes for ease, for beauty, and for interest!"

His observations still hold true. Lucca is full of historical delights and mercifully less over-run with visitors than Florence, its big sister to the south. The city is well-mannered, wealthy and welcoming, with lots of pretty parks, romantic piazzas, churches and venerable palazzi, all set within Renaissance walls.

Locanda L'Elisa is one of Tuscany's finest hotels, one of Relais et Châteaux's gems. It blends the beauties of the old with the conveniences of the new, and does so with panache. The entire building, for instance, is air-conditioned in full summer, a great relief for the traveller, like myself, arriving hot, tired and dusty at its doors.

It offers just eight suites, a double room and one single, so booking well ahead is recommended.

The restoration of Locanda L'Elisa has been impeccable, inside and out... the gardens, especially, are a delight, full of colour and unexpected features. The swimming-pool meanders like a natural lake and plump green trees and swathes of summery blossoms are magically reflected in its waters.

The atmosphere at Locanda L'Elisa is more that of a genteel country villa than a bustling hotel; a homely sense of peace and good living is everywhere. You'll find bowls of fresh fruit and vases of scented flowers in your room, and there's a cosy lounge and a glittering conservatory, where the evening meal is served.

As you'd expect, the food is delicious, the freshest local produce cooked to perfection to mouth-watering traditional Tuscan recipes, accompanied by an extensive, well-chosen wine list.

I spent a happy evening secluded within the walls of Locanda L'Elisa, enjoying the gardens, lit by and almost full moon rising in a cloudless sky. Next morning, after a wonderful breakfast, I set out to walk the walls of Lucca's old town. It was a glorious Sunday morning, and in the Piazza San Martino, I came across an open-air antiques market. I spent an hour rummaging from stall to stall. Thankfully, for I had more travelling to do, I came away with nothing but fond memories.

La Collegiata

Originally, La Collegiata was a monastery belonging to the Capucine monks of the Franciscan order, built in the middle of the 16th century. It stands high on a hill, surrounded by luscious green cypresses, with a splendid view of the towers of San Gimignano. The wonderful old building, with its elegant proportions and its walls in soft-coloured stone so typical of the area, has been sympathetically restored to retain its historic and sober beauty. Yet, it has all the luxuries a modern traveller could wish for, and much more... After you have settled into your cosy room and admired the view from the balcony, you'll soon be lured outside to wander in the fabulous gardens, stroll through the park or take a leisurely swim in the luxurious open-air swimming pool. The building itself is steeped in a history to equal that of San Gimignano itself. It has a tranquil courtyard with an enchanting well, shadowy cloisters where you can take refuge from the sun in the heat of the day, and a little chapel where you can spend some peaceful moments of reverie.

The rooms and suites in the hotel, 20 in all, are spacious and oak-beamed, with lovely carpets and antique furniture, each of them different, each of them equally delightful. In the vaulted, high-ceilinged restaurant, friendly waiters serve the very best of local specialities, accompanied by the glorious wines that make the region famous. La Collegiata exudes such tranquility and beauty that it would be very tempting to just stay here, enjoying the sunshine and slow, long walks in the environment, but if you wish, San Gimignano can easily be reached by car or, if you have more energy, even on foot. There, you can enjoy the beauty of this delightful town that has no equal anywhere in the world, and admire its towers, its wonderful streets, romantic alleyways and interesting little shops. Later, you will be happy to return to your peaceful home away from home at La Collegiata, and be grateful that, all those years ago, the people of San Gimignano asked for this monastery to be built.

Il Pellicano

It started out as a routine flight, such as British aviator Michael Graham had made so often before. But in a matter of seconds, it changed into a nightmare. The plane was in trouble and it was going to crash in the heart of the African bush. There seemed no escape.

Michael had no time to ponder, no time to calculate the risk. He had nothing – except the choice between certain death and one slight chance of saving his life. He took that chance – and jumped. Without a parachute, with nothing but the wild hope that the dense foliage below would prevent him from crashing to the ground.

Who says that miracles never happen? Michael Graham landed safely, the sole survivor of that devastating crash. He lived to tell the tale, newspapers were keen to take up his story.

In the United States, Patsy Daszel read about the brave Englishman, and longed to meet him. For a second time, luck was on their side: years later, by total coincidence, Michael and Patsy met at a Californian promontory named Pelican Point. And so began a love story that is still firmly alive at Il Pellicano.

From then, Patsy and Michael were inseparable. Together, they travelled all over Europe, in search of a place as fascinating and special as the love between them. One day they found it, in the wilds of Monte Argentario, on a rocky headland with stunning sea views, facing out towards Corsica. There they built a villa as an ode to their love. Today, over 30 years later, it is a world-class hotel, with a guest list to match.

I arrived at the hottest hour in the middle of one of the hottest day of summer. Il Pellicano, its terracotta roofs nestling among gnarled pines and ancient olive trees, looked cool and inviting, the creeper-laden arches of the front porch welcoming me into the reception room. I sank gratefully into one of the comfortable sofas waiting there for road-weary travellers like myself. Further arches led into deeper shadows within.

My luxurious room was one of the 16 double rooms in the main building, but there are no less than seven cottages on the Il Pellicano estate, where the eight junior suites and six deluxe suites are situated. After a rest, I took a walk around my new home. Below the pool with its entourage of white parasols, lay the ever-changing sea. A lizard scuttled from under my feet and disappeared in the undergrowth. The air was heavy with the scent of wild herbs.

I had heard, already, that dinner would be something very special at Il Pellicano. And it was. The combination of fine food and wonderful wines, moonlight on the water and the warm glow of the lamp on my table on the terrace made me feel utterly, romantic, deeply at peace with the world and myself. This, is told myself, is pure bliss.

And I resolved to do nothing at all that evening, possibly not even tomorrow. Other guests might rush off to do scuba diving, water-skiing, taking part in the many delights this hotel has to offer. But I would just sit here – and enjoy the magic legacy of two lovers Lady Luck had smiled on.

Relais La Suvera

It is late afternoon in a Sienese autumn and the castle is filling with long shadows. The 16th century is still young, and there is news, from travellers and passing merchants, of great doings in the world. A voice calls and another, further away, answers. Otherwise, there is silence. A gray cat stretches elegantly, trots away purposefully through an open stable door.

All at once, there is a bubbubb at the castle gate. A clattering of hooves, shouts. Figures appear at high windows, curious to see who these new arrivals might be. A day earlier than expected, the great architect Baldassarre Peruzzi has arrived from Rome! There is much to-ing and fro-ing as a suitable welcome is prepared for the great man. It is the beginning of sweeping changes in the already ancient face of the castle of La Suvera. For many months, there will be no peace, as stonemasons, carpenters and artisans of all kinds chip, saw and hammer, as they bring to life the Renaissance visions of the celebrated architect.

Even today, here at La Suvera, history lives on, blends with legend. Centuries before Peruzzi's visit, the Knights Templar had a centre here, a fortress and a stagingpost. Distinguished counts were named as owners of La Suvera, Pope Julius II – indeed, it was none other than he who called on Peruzzi to 'modernise' La Suvera in the style of his times.

Today it is the country residence of the Marquis Ricci and his wife Princess Massimo. It is they who have created, here at La Suvera, an hotel of unique elegance and great historical significance. It is not simply one building, but more an entire village, a community of buildings, a church, a stable block, an olive press house and the principal edifice, the Papal Villa. All of it standing no distance at all from such medieval gems as many-towered San Gimignano, Casole d'Elsa and Monteriggioni, on a hill overlooking a gorgeous stretch of typical Tuscan countryside between Florence and Siena.

The Marquis and his wife have created 35 air-conditioned rooms and suites here, some to be found in each of the principal buildings. Every one is a world of its own, like a page from a history book. Precious heirlooms dedicated to a particular period are to be found in the rooms, and all the furniture is so perfectly in the style of that period that it is almost a surprise to see that every modern comfort is available too.

I strolled from the Italian gardens that encircle the buildings into the private vineyards beyond, and watched grapes being plucked that will make this year's fine wines. That evening in the 'Oliviera' restaurant, set in the ancient olive-pressing house, I sipped a glass of the Marquis's own Riserva Giulio II. And for a few moments imagined that I was myself an honoured and noble guest, resting on my way between prestigious appointments.

After my meal, I found my way to the library and sat with a heavy volume of poems on my lap, watching night fall, watching a little gray kitten leap up onto a windowsill. Was she a descendant, by some wild chance, of that cat who, from the safety of the stables, heard the noisome arrival of the architect Peruzzi, so long ago?

Castello di Magona

Less than 200 years ago, Italy was still a collection of fractious separate kingdoms, or Grand Duchys, and Tuscany was one such, with important cities not long incorporated within it - Florence, Lucca, Siena and Pisa.
Leopold II became Grand Duke of Tuscany in 1824, following the death of his father. Castello di Magona was one of the principal residences he inherited. The Maremma, now a fertile grassland plain on Italy's western coast, was once only a swamp; Leopold instigated much useful drainage work and used nearby Magona as his home.

The castle passed into private hands in 1860 and has remained in the care of the same family ever since. Today, fortunate travellers can share the elegant and exclusive castle with them. There are just four suites, one rather special 'Grand Duke' bedroom and three twin-bedded rooms. In the summer months, a cool and welcoming swimming-pool, set alluringly under the protective shade of great leafy trees, awaits the travel-worn guest.

I arrived late afternoon at Castello di Magona, after a busy and exhausting stay in Florence, and found it a welcome change to be in such a peaceful hillside retreat. I was met in the cool entrance hall by the charming host himself and we chatted under the sternly enigmatic gaze of a pair of suits of armour.

Once settled in my air-conditioned room, with its radiant views, lovely antique furnishings, cosy bathroom and thick, protective stone walls, I changed and set out eagerly for the pool, which I had all to myself. I found time to lie in the sun, take a relaxing stroll around the grounds, and have a leisurely drink in the lounge before sitting down to a dinner that would put many a five-star establishment to shame.

The desk had informed me they could help organise any number of excursions for me. I could tour Pisa, Lucca or Siena (none were too far off) or take to the sea by private boat and view Elba close up. I could visit wine cellars in the area, or play golf or tennis. The Palio, Siena's extraordinary urban horse race, was still weeks away... but even that would not have been for me. I love discovering those little-known villages that escape popular tourism, and had been told of one such place some ten miles east of Massa Maritima.

Just a year before, I'd spent several fascinating days scrambling amongst the 'perched villages' of the Alpes Maritimes, behind Nice - and Roccatederighi, I was assured, would match any of them. It was, indeed, a delightful find. The alleys are steep as cliff faces, but my efforts were amply rewarded with the best views anywhere of the grassy Maremma.

103

The Castello di Magona is an ideal home for anyone keen to absorb the romance and visual beauty of medieval Tuscan towns and villages such as Campiglia Maritima, Suvereto, Bolgheri and Castagneto Carducci.

I hadn't left myself time to visit all of these, but I knew I would return to Magona, to renew the friendships I made there, to taste the sublime food... and discover new secrets.

107

Certosa di Maggiano

There is great pleasure to be had, of course, from visiting ancient buildings, religious and secular, in wonderfully romantic cities like Sienna... but imagine you were able to actually spend a few days and nights living in such a place. The Hotel Certosa di Maggiano makes such a dream attainable.

If you are sufficiently sharp-eyed, as you wander the storied shadows of Siena's magnificent Cathedral, you might come across the beautifully-sculpted tomb of one Riccardo Petroni. It was Cardinal Petroni, who in his will, dated 1314, left a large sum for the construction of a monastery in Siena for the Carthusian monks. His son Pietro, just 17, was later to enter the order and resided in the completed monastery.

Time, the ravages of war and even earthquake and fire have, over the centuries, destroyed all of the original building except the cloisters and the ancient belltower. Much rebuilding at various times and, latterly, many ill-conceived renovations and alterations left the essential beauty of the original edifice hidden.

In the 1960s, it was purchased by heart surgeon Professor Adalberto Grossi and his wife Anna Recordati. Chiefly due to her vision and enthusiasm, the property was carefully and sympathetically restored, and it opened as an hotel in 1975. Three years later it became a member of the renowned Relais & Chateaux Association.

Today, as one steps into the magnificent courtyard, the serenity of its ancient monastic past is still palpable. The outside world was held at arm's length for the duration of my stay. Breakfast in the comfortable old Tuscan kitchen, a light lunch at a table set in the old open 14th century cloister, looking out onto the twinkling swimming pool, a stroll across the lawns, through the well-stocket kitchen gardens, which provide much of the fresh food for the hotel kitchen, and out into the olive groves beyond... I marvelled that I was still so close to the centre of Siena, and decided to do some serious sightseeing the next day.

Next morning, I found myself on the Piazza del Campo, the most beautiful piazza in Italy. Once, executions and bull fights took place here, and today, it is still the scene of the famous Palio, when jockeys on unsaddled horses race each other and many bets are closed on who the winner might be. Restaurants, cafés and beautiful medieval palazzi line the Campo, and I admired the impressive Palazzo Pubblico and the delightful Torre del Mangia. After long hours exploring the streets and squares, it was wonderful to step into my own suite, to soak in a deep bath in the luxuriously appointed bathroom and to relax, before dinner, on my own private roof terrace, caressed by a soft warm breeze.

Throughout the hotel, paintings and antiques of great beauty catch the eye – in the reception hall, in the elegant dining room where I enjoyed a delightful, very Italian meal, in each of the bedrooms and suites. Beauty seems a natural part of Certosa di Maggiano, as it is of Siena.

La Frateria di Padre Eligio

Among the peaceful, deeply-wooded hills of Monte Cetano, on the border of Tuscany and its equally lovely neighbour Umbria, lay the ruins of a friary founded in 1212 by St. Francis himself. Centuries later, a Franciscan brother, Padre Eligio, created a community here of young people who set aside their troubled pasts to join together in rebuilding and restoring the tumbledown buildings almost from scratch.

Today, La Frateria, or Brotherhood, of Padre Eligio have achieved their great ambition - the Convento di San Francesco is a serene and beautiful refuge, a three-star hotel of quite surprising quality with just seven guest rooms.

It is still employing the same kind of troubled youngsters, whose work under the guidance of Father Eligio has transformed the delapidated buildings.

The bread, the olive oil, the vegetables and herbs, even the meat served at your table are grown and produced right here, or else at another of Padre Eligio's communities.

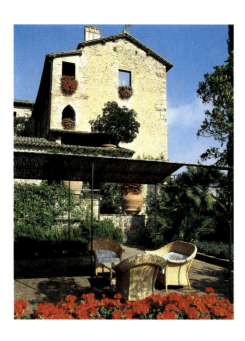

What I appreciated as much as anything at this very special refuge is that it is as much a monastery as it is an hotel. There is a chapel still dedicated to quietude and prayer... there are sunlit courtyards, a bell tower and shadow-filled cloisters where you might expect, at any moment, a sandalled friar to pas you by with downcast eyes. My spacious and simply-furnished room had the grave and peaceful atmosphere of a monk's cell.

I loved it here. By day, I took myself off on foot into the surrounding countryside, returning only as the late afternoon sun turned the tall westward-facing walls a glowing rose colour. By night, I combined an excellent dinner, graciously served, with a walk around the grounds, and enjoyed a fascinating conversation with Father Eligio himself.

I left regretfully. And as I drove away, I thought that St. Francis may no longer be found in person at the Convento di San Francesco, but his spirit of kindliness and peacefulness lives on.

Gallery Hotel Art

It could be said there are two Italies, both as alluring as one another - an ancient Italy of wonderful medieval buildings and world-famous masterpieces and sculptures, and a contemporary Italy of cutting-edge architecture, avant-garde art and designer fashion houses.

In Florence, you can immerse yourself in both these exciting worlds simply by booking a room or suite in what is both a gallery (of ever-changing top quality works from modern art and photography to ethnic design and traditional antiques) and a designer hotel to equal any in London, New York or Los Angeles. All this, a stone's throw from the lively sun-sparkling River Arno hurrying under the Ponte Vecchio westward to the sea.

Walk into the amazing lobby of Gallery Hotel Art and you will be entranced by the clean, spare design of the huge, airy space and by the stunning red or black lacquered Burmese antiques. Not only is the Hotel Art a meeting-place between old and new, it is a tasteful fusion, too, of East and West. The library, the breakfast room and the American bar - all three are unforgettable.

Beautiful as each individual object is, and however clever the understated use of colour might be, it is the magical lighting that, above all else, gives Gallery Hotel Art its entirely original and serene, subtle yet dynamic atmosphere.

After its complete renovation (the overall responsibility of gifted architect Michele Bonan and the Salvatore Ferragamo group), the hotel re-opened in 1999, to great acclaim. It was envisaged as an aesthetic and exciting meeting-place and home from home for the sophisticated international traveller and his friends and colleagues... and it has succeeded beyond all expectations.

The 65 luxurious rooms and stunning suites are, each of them, peaceful refuges from the busy world outside. They are air-conditioned, have fax and modem facilities, satellite Bang and Olufsen televisions and video conferencing.

If you require to be whisked across Florence in comfort, you can call on the services of a chauffeured limousine. I should imagine Botticelli himself would wish he could transport his spirit from the walls of the Uffizi to a place of his own at the magnificent Gallery Hotel Art!

Villa San Michele

The Medici family have a secure place in history. But 15th century Italy had a second family of a wealth to rival the Medicis: the Davanzatis. And it was to this family I owed my short but spectacular journey out of the heat and bustle of Florence, up into the hills towards Fiesole. It they had not, in 1411, donated a portion of land there to the Franciscans, I would not be making my way now to one of the most exquisite hotels in the whole of Italy.

The oratory the monks built there, as a place of prayer dedicated to the archangel Michael, was expanded, again by the generosity of the Davenzatis, into a monastery. No less an artist than Michelangelo was commissioned to design the colonnaded façade, which is such a beautiful feature of the villa. As time went by, hermits and monks gave way to secular personages, who made vague and piecemeal attempts at renovation, then to men of action – to soldiers of Napoleon's army, to occupying officers of first the German, then the Allied forces. It was even vacant, on occasion, and bombarded. But now the long-suffering 15th century villa is enjoying a second heyday. The complete restoration that was its due has been triumphantly achieved, at great cost, and Villa San Michele is now a listed Italian National Trust monument and an oasis for those who long for peace and quiet.

On my arrival at the villa, I was courteously greeted and shown first to the registration desk, set in the lobby that was previously a 15th century chapel. It was pointed out to me that the telephone booth nearby had once been a confessional.

Such little delights and surprises are everywhere; a triptych in the lounge that might have found a place in the Uffizi, a fresco of the Last Supper by Ferrucci on the library ceiling, two little chapels of prayer, a secluded inner courtyard that seemed to glow still with the simple piety of centuries past, curious little twisting staircases leading up to rooms wih fourposter beds, clay urns of fresh flowers, antique desks and wardrobes, and bathrooms with jacuzzis and marbled bathtubs.

Apart from mealtimes, my fellow guests were seldom to be encountered, although you can count on the hotel being fully booked at all times. Their presence is soon lost in the extensive gardens, or in the stunning loggia. Many guests use the San Michele as a base to visit he city, and free transport is provided for them. But I was happy to stay here. I strolled from terrace to terrace, discovered an enthusiastic waterfall, a serene pool full of blue and green reflections, romantic shawls of climbing roses and wisteria that made waterfalls of their own. Beyond, footpaths wandered into piney woods and led me, beneath cypresses and olives, up into Fiesole itself.

Dining at Villa San Michele is pure delight. The intimate Cenacolo Restaurant, hung with tapestries and old Italian paintings and dominated by a huge stone fireplace, is brough to life by the shifting lights of candles. The menu and the wine list make choosing almost impossible. I opted for succulent game and wild mushrooms, a Florentine steak, a meringue with wild strawberries... With a glass of the Villa's own label Chianti, I toasted the generosity of the Davanzatis, and my own good fortune to have discovered this delightful hotel.

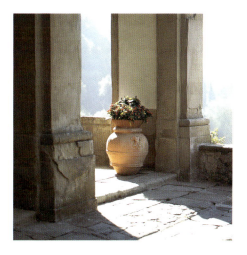

Relais Villa Arceno

Two limousines drive through a discreet entrance gate and follow a winding unpaved road, flanked by venerable cypresses, through an exquisite private estate. They stop in front of a magnificent 17th century yellow-ochre villa set on a low hill. Almost simultaneously Chrysler's top man Lee Iaccoca and Luca di Montezemolo, head of Ferrari, step out of their cars and greet each other. Nearby, an old gardener is more interested in watering the lawn than in the meeting of these two illustrious men. Lee and Luca stroll towards the terrace, where cool champagne is set out for them, sparkling in the morning sunshine. The sound of crickets and birds drowns their voices and a couple of hours later, after an extensive lunch, they end their meeting with a firm handshake. The two cars drive away again, into the Tuscan countryside, one to the north, the other to the south.

In Italy, there are still exclusive places like this, where more high-level political decisions are made, more top business deals concluded than in Senate commissions or the headquarters of multinational companies. Hotel Relais Villa Arceno is one such place. It was built in 1671, and for centuries, it was the privileged living quarters of aristocratic families. The Villa is surrounded by wonderful Italian gardens, which were designed by Agostino Fantastici - a very suitable name. But there is more. Arceno used to be the centre of a gigantic agricultural group consisting of 33 farms, most of which have now been extensively renovated and sold or rented to rich people from the city. The proud owner of this unique refined hotel which overlooks the rolling hills of the Chianti region is Gualtieri Mancini. When we met him, just before we left, he gave us the following tips: "Do come back in July, when we celebrate the 'New Moon' and the 'Harvest Festival' in the hotel and in the village - it is something you will never forget! In the evening, there is traditional dancing to accordion music, and we sing traditional songs. And if you can't make it in July, any other summer month will do, for then we organise evening concerts by the Accademia Chigiana from Siena in the gardens of the Villa."

Helvetia & Bristol

The curiously-named Helvetia and Bristol is situated in the very heart of ancient Florence, halfway between the Palazzo del Duomo and the romantic River Arno. From its front doors, almost every famous landmark is within easy walking distance.

Florence is the undisputed cradle of the Renaissance. In the 14th and 15th centuries, with the encouragement of the ruling Medici family, a climate grew that favoured a veritable explosion not only of the arts but culture in general. Cosimo was an enthusiastic patron of both sculptors and painters, he ordered frescoes form Fra Angelico and is credited with discovering the genius of sculptor Donatello. All the richer Florentine families of the period supported the goldsmiths, the potters and the weavers of silk and sumptuous brocades. Scholars chased from Constantinople by marauding Turks found safe refuge in Florence and contributed to the city's incomparable legacy. Paintings, sculptures, frescoes, superb architecture, cobbled alleyways, arched streets and wonderfully romantic bridges like the Ponte Vecchio lure hundreds upon thousands of visitors a year from all over the world.

After a long day exploring Florence, it is a great relish to step into the five-star luxury of the Helvetia and Bristol. The hotel was completely restored during the 1980s and fits seamlessly into its historic surroundings. It sits, elegant and tranquil; on the Via Pescioni, oppposite the Palazzo Strozzi, a wonderfully compelling combination of olde worlde luxury, graceful hospitality and every sophisticated modern convenience.

Wherever you look, gorgeous antiques catch the eye, fine capets and exquisite furniture, collected over the years with discrimination.
Its arresting name can be easily explained: the original owners were a Swiss family, and Bristol was added later to give the hotel's name a more familiar ring to English travellers.
The hotel offers 52 palatial rooms, furnished with sofas and armchairs of thick velvet, strewn with glowing oriental rugs and graced with bathrooms in Carrera marble. In the suites and de luxe double rooms you'll discover your own jaccuzi waiting to soothe away all your stresses and aches.

There is the Winter Garden café bar, a great place for meeting up with friends, and the Bristol Restaurant for a truly gourmet experience, overseen by chef Francesco Casu, who uses the best of local seasonal produce to create a modern culinary experience based on Tuscan tradicional recipes.
After your meal, take a stroll down to the banks of the darkly sparkling Arno, rolling silently and mysteriously by, or have a nightcap at an open-air café on the Piazza della Republica. Lasting memories can sometimes be so simply made.

Castello di Montegufoni

Set conveniently close to the great city of Florence, yet at the same time beautifully rural, Montegufoni is a wonderful alternative to the grand hotel experience, offering whole families the chance to gather together, cook for themselves, and discover Tuscany at their own pace.

The castle has a story that goes back far beyond the 12th century. It was owned by the Ormani family, mentioned by name in Dante's Divine Comedy; it was destroyed by warring Florentines in 1135; lay in abject ruin for 70 years, was rebuilt and became a small but influential hamlet of seven houses surrounded by great defensive walls. It saw kings, dukes and cardinals come and go and during the Renaissance it became a haunt of artists, poets and sculptors. For 300 long years it

remained a salon of repute, falling gradually into graceful decline, until George Sitwell discovered it, fell in love with it, and purchased it for his son Osbert.

Many costly improvements were made and Montegufoni reclaimed its past splendours. It is this building, further restored by current proprietor Sergio Posarelli, that welcomes you today, with the sonorous and formal gravity of its medieval shadows and the happy pleasures of its supremely peaceful setting, in the very heartland of Tuscany.

The castle offers a selection of 15 wonderful apartments, so spacious they can accommodate not just two, but five, and even eight people. Each is named, which emphasises their individuality but goes only some way to encompassing their comfort and grandeur.

Each apartment is beautiful in its own right, but the most prestigious, La Galleria, sleeps eight in comfort and takes up an entire wing in the castle; it has its own kitchen, of course, but also no less than six French windows that open onto the pretty landscaped gardens, and a balcony that overlooks the pleasing formality of the monastery-like central courtyard.

Beyond the castello, like so many offspring, are ten villas, also very beautiful, so Montegufori is, once more, the hamlet it was so many centuries ago.

You will find a tavern-style restaurant in the castle grounds, offering Tuscan fare as good as you might find anywhere, and there is a bar, too, doubling as a useful shop to pick up those basic necessities.

Florentines would do wel to consider invading Montegufoni once again, but as appreciative guests, this time!

151

It is this castle that welcomes you today with the sonorous and formal gravity of its medieval shadows.

Hotel J&J

Firenze is without doubt the town in Italy which most intensely exudes the atmosphere of the country. In order to understand the soul of this town, you need days, even weeks. Its wealth, beauty and culture is overwhelming, so much so that, if you don't take your time, you will find it hard to distinguish between its paintings, statues, squares, palaces, streets, shops and restaurants. The ideal place to stay during a longer visit to Firenze is Hotel J&J, where within its venerable walls, you remain in touch with all the beauty you have seen during the day. The 16th century Renaissance palace in the Santa Croce district, no more than five minutes walk from attractions like the Piazza del

Duomo with its monumental cathedral, the Loggia della Signoria, Palazzo Vecchia, Piazza della Signoria, the Ponte Vecchio and the silver river Arno, still retains its original frescoes, stucco and includes an exquisite monastery with Doric columns. Each of the rooms, some of which are real lofts, are furnished with precious antiques. Some look out over the idyllic courtyard, others over the red rooftops of the old town. And many have a small private terrace, original frescoes and decorative mouldings. Breakfast is served in the vaulted room of the former monastery, and after that, you are free to discover the gastronomic delights of Florence itself. In this hotel, you truly do live in Renaissance Italy.

Locanda dell'Amorosa

Amorosa is much more than just an hotel. As I approached, it was nestling on the low skyline in a throng of dark green cypresses, and its cluster of buildings, tall and imposing even from a distance, looked more like a little village. Which, indeed, it once was, with a recorded history going back to the 14th century. But during its painstaking restoration, archeological finds included pieces of an infinitely older Etruscan temple.

Today, the Amorosa estate is part of the larger village of Sinalunga, set in a flat and fertile valley that once was a swamp, originally drained by the inventive Etruscans, and then drained again some 200 years ago, to provide, today, wonderful land for the much-prized Florentine bistecca cattle, for extensive vineyards and groves of olives.

Sinalunga lies halfway between Siena and San Gimignano, to the west, and Perugia and Assisi, to the east. Amorosa, therefore, is well placed as a base for enjoying this wonderful region of Tuscany.

I found my way to the entrance of Locanda dell'Amorosa by way of a long avenue of cypress trees. An ancient brick archway opened onto a big Renaissance piazza, around which the buildings are disposed.
Amorosa was a farm, housing not only the farmer's family and the animals, but all the farm workers, too. Even today, the hotel is only part of a larger endeavour that includes wine, an exclusive extra virgin olive oil, sunflowers and grain.

I wandered through gardens, into woodlands, alongside the yellow meadows of nodding sunflowers, and between neat rows of ripening vines. I felt totally immersed in the true and vibrant life of Tuscany.

There is a wonderfully rustic atmosphere even in the spacious guest rooms; warm, characterful peasant furniture mixes happily with quality antiques and good paintings, and with all the usual modern conveniences: big, comfortable beds, fine bathrooms and air-conditioning.

The ancient, vaulted restaurant, with its pretty brick pillars, is a wonderful place to linger over breakfast, savour fresh Italian patisserie and drink a strong tasty coffee after an excellent dinner.

The cuisine is a modern take on traditional Tuscan recipes, a credit to youthful chef Walter Redaelli. The wine list is strong on good Italian wines in general, and regional wines in particular, and includes the three created right here at Amorosa. When I left, I knew that the Locanda dell'Amorosa would always have a special place in my heart.

Villa Vignamaggio

La Gioconda, painted by Leonardo da Vinci and now hanging in the illustrious Louvre, in Paris, is better known to us as the Mona Lisa. The subject of his painting was a real person, the daughter of Anton Gherardini... and, in 1479, she was born right here at Vignamaggio. The villa is 100 years and more older than she, and has survived with the same tenacity, care and good fortune as the lady of the famously inscrutable smile.

Vignamaggio, which translates loosely as 'the wines of May', is a working farm, a wine-producing estate, and it presses its own high quality olive oil. It can be found in the heart of Chianti, a few miles south and west of Greve, chief town of the famous Chianti Classico, or Gallo Nero, wine region - and, as you might expect, it is surrounded by extensive vineyards, and by olive groves.

Vignamaggio has a further, more recently won, claim to fame. It was chosen by Kenneth Branagh as the real-life film set of his version of Shakespeare's Much Ado About Nothing. It isn't an hotel, but offers a clutch of luxury self-catering suites, so you will have to rely on finding suitable eating houses in the area, which will not, in fact, be particularly difficult, for there are a good few very reasonable ones nearby. I'd suggest you try Da Verrazzano, an hotel, which has a popular restaurant with a considerable local reputation.

What else will you find to enjoy at Vignamaggio? There are swimming pools, tennis courts, a safe playground for young children, and a fitness centre. It makes a good base for exploring not only the immediate Chianti region and its dozens of vineyards, but really, the whole of Tuscany is within striking distance. Florence is maybe an hour to the north; Siena, to the south, will take much the same time, without having to rush it.

But I'd be all for a less punishing schedule. Between the Florence to Siena 'superstrada' eastwards and the fierce Autostrada del Sole to the west, is a whole network of country roads waiting to be discovered and enjoyed. Pick up bread, cheese, olives and a good local wine, find a shady and secluded spot, and have a picnic on the grass. Simple pleasures often make for the best memories. The Chianti region is often thought of as beautiful Tuscany, distilled. See if you think the same.

Useful information

RELAIS IL FALCONIERE pag. 10
Localita S.Martino 370
52044 Cortona
Ph.. (39) 0575 61 26 16
Fax (39) 0575 61 29 27
e-Mail : falconiere@relaischateaux.fr
Website : www.relaischateaux.fr/falconiere

SALVADONICA pag. 18
Val di Pesa
50024 Mercantale/ Firenze
Ph. (39) 055 821 80 39
Fax (39) 055 821 80 43
e-Mail : salvadonica@tin.it
Website : www.cosmos.it/business/salvadonica

CASTELLETTO DI MONTEBENICHI pag. 24
52020 Montebenichi-Bucine (Arezzo)
Ph. (39) 055 99 10 110
Fax (39) 055 99 10 113
e-Mail : monteben@val.it
Website : www.val.it/hotel/castelletto

L'ANTICO POZZO pag. 30
Via San Matteo 87
53037 San Gimignano
Ph. (39) 0577 94 20 14
Fax (39) 0577 94 21 17
e-Mail : info@anticopozzo.com
Website : www.anticopozzo.com

LUCIGNANELLO BANDINI pag. 34
Lucignano d'Asso
53020 San Giovanni d'Asso/ Siena
Ph. (39) 0577 80 30 68
Fax (39) 0577 80 30 82
e-Mail : piccolomini@commune.siena.it
Website : www.nautilus-mp.com/piccolomininaldi

L'OLMO pag. 42
53020 Monticchiello di Pienza/ Siena
Ph. (39) 0578 755 133
Fax (39) 0578 755 124
e-Mail : flindo@tin.it
Website : www.nautilus-mp.com/olmo

LUNGARNO pag. 48
Borgo Sant'Jacopo
50125 Firenze
Ph. (39) 055 27 261
Fax (39) 055 26 84 37
Website www.lungarnohotels.com
e-Mail : bookings@lungarnohotels.com

IL BOTACCIO DI MONTIGNOSO pag. 54
Via Bottaccio 1
54038 Montignoso
Ph. (39) 0585 34 00 31
Fax (39) 0585 34 01 03
e-Mail bottaccio@relaischateaux.fr
Website : www.relaischateaux.fr/bottaccio

VILLA LA MASSA pag. 60
Via La Massa 6
50010 Firenze/ Candeli
Ph. (39) 055 62 611
Fax (39) 055 63 31 02
e-Mail : lamassa@relaischateaux.fr
Website : www.relaischateaux.fr/lamassa

BORGO ARGENINA pag. 68
Argenina
53013 Gaiole in Chianti/ Siena
Ph. (39) 0577 74 71 17
Fax (39) 0577 74 71 17
Website : www.chiantinet.it/argenina

LOCANDA L'ELISA pag. 76
Via Nuova per Pisa 1952
55050 Lucca
Ph. (39) 0583 37 97 37
Fax (39) 0583 37 90 19
e-Mail : elisa@relaischateaux.fr
Website : www.relaischateaux.fr/elisa

LA COLLEGIATA pag. 80
Loc. Strada 27
53037 San Gimignano
Ph. (39) 0577 94 32 01
Fax (39) 0577 94 05 66
e-Mail : collegiata@relaischateaux.fr
Website : www.relaischateaux.fr/collegiata

IL PELLICANO pag. 86
Cala dei Santi
58018 Porto Ercole, Grosseto
Ph. (39) 0564 85 81 11
Fax (39) 0564 83 34 18
e-Mail : pellicano@relaischateaux.fr
Website : www.relaischateaux.fr/pellicano

RELAIS LA SUVERA pag. 92
53030 Pievescola di Casole d'Elsa
Ph. (39) 0577 96 03 00
Fax (39) 0577 96 02 20
e-Mail : lasuvera@lasuvera.it
Website : www.lasuvera.it

CASTELLO DI MAGONA pag. 100
57021 Campiglia Marittima/ Livorno
Ph. (39) 0565 85 12 35
Fax (39) 0565 85 51 27
e-Mail : relais@castellodimagona.it
Website : www.castellodimagona.it

CERTOSA DI MAGGIANO pag. 108
Strada di Certosa 82
53100 Siena
Ph. (39) 0577 28 81 80
Fax (39) 0577 28 81 89
e-Mail : certosa@relaischateaux.fr
Website : www.relaischateaux.fr/certosa

LA FRATERIA DI PADRE ELIGIO pag. 116
Convento San Francesco
53040 Cetona
Ph.(39) 0578 23 80 15
Fax (39) 0578 239 220
e-Mail : frateria@ftbcc.it

GALLERY HOTEL ART pag. 122
Vicolo dell'Oro 5
50123 Firenze
Ph. (39) 055 27 263
Fax (39) 055 26 85 57
e-Mail : gallery@lungarnohotels.com

VILLA SAN MICHELE pag. 128
Via Doccia 4
50014 Firenze
Ph. (39) 055 567 82 00
Fax (39) 567 82 50
e-Mail : reservations@villasanmichele.net

RELAIS VILLA ARCENO pag. 134
53010 San Gusmè
Castelnuovo Berardenga/ Siena
Ph. (39) 0577 35 92 92
Fax (39) 0577/ 35 92 76

HELVETIA & BRISTOL pag. 140
Via dei Pescioni 2
50123 Firenze
Ph. (39) 055 28 78 14
Fax (39) 055 28 83 53
e-Mail : hbf@charminghotels.it
Website : www.charminghotels.it/helvetia

CASTELLO DI MONTEGUFONI pag. 146
50020 Montagnana/ Firenze
Ph. (39) 0571 67 11 31
Fax (39) 0571 6 7 15 14
e-Mail : mgufini@sienanet.it

HOTEL J & J pag. 154 Via di Mezzo 20 50121 Firenze Ph. (39) 055 26 31 21 Fax (39) 055 24 02 82 e-Mail : jandi@dada.it Website : www.jandjhotel.com	**LOCANDA DELL'AMOROSA** pag. 158 L'Amorosa 53048 Sinalunga/ Siena Ph. (39) 0577 67 94 97 Fax (39) 0577 63 20 01 e-Mail : locanda@amorosa.it Website : www.amorosa.it	**VILLA VIGNAMAGGIO** pag. 166 55022 Greve in Chianti Ph. (39) 055 85 46 61 Fax (39) 055 85 44 368 e-Mail : agriturismo@vignamaggio.com Website : www.vignamaggio.com

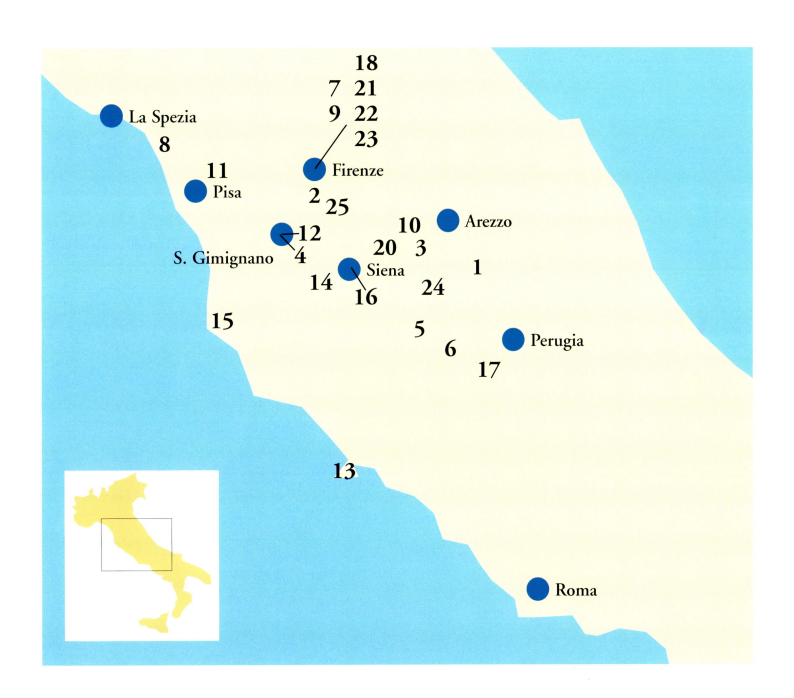

Published in this series

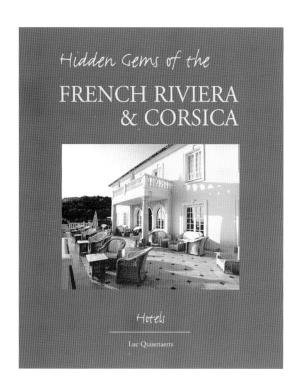
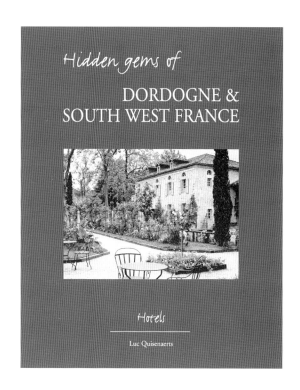

More information on all our books you find on our website:
www.d-publications.com